Angels i.. ...

Elaine Murray Stone
Cathy Rayburn

Paulist Press
New York/Mahwah, N.J.

Cover and interior illustrations by Frank Sabatté
Cover design by Sharyn Banks
Book design by Lynn Else

Library of Congress Cataloging-in-Publication Data

Stone, Elaine Murray, 1922-
  Angels in the Bible / Elaine Murray Stone, Cathy Rayburn.
      p. cm.
    ISBN 0-8091-6729-8 (alk. paper)
    1. Angels—Biblical teaching—Juvenile literature. 2. Bible stories, English. I. Rayburn, Cathy. II. Title.
    BS680.A48S76 2006
    235′.3—dc22

                                                                            200501782

Published by Paulist Press
997 Macarthur Boulevard
Mahwah, New Jersey 07430

www.paulistpress.com

Printed and bound in the
United States of America

Contents

Angels in the Old Testament

Angels in the New Testament

To Ella Felice,
our own little angel

Introduction:
Who and What Are
Angels?

Angels are spiritual beings, messengers of God. God uses angels to send announcements and warnings to his people, or to help or protect them in time of trouble or danger.

When people wanted to draw these messengers, they imagined that angels needed a way to travel from heaven to earth. That is why angels are often shown with wings. But real angels are pure spirit. They have no body—and no wings.

Each angel is considered to be an individual person, and many have been given names. The best known are the archangels Gabriel, Raphael, and Michael, who are mentioned by name in the Old and New Testaments. Archangels are angels with a higher rank, a chief angel. Tradition says that there are seven archangels allowed to enter the glory of the Lord. There they bring our prayers to God.

God has given each of us an angel to guard and guide us. These are known as "guardian" angels and protect us from harm, sickness, and injury. Guardian angels might protect someone in battle, or help him or her escape an accident. They also help guide our minds toward God and away from evil.

Are angels male or female? The names of the most famous angels are masculine, yet paintings of angels often show them as female. However, because angels are spirits, they have no sex and real angels are neither male nor female.

Are angels always good? No. According to scripture, some angels sinned terribly and were cast out of heaven. The sin usually mentioned is that of pride. Satan is the chief of the fallen angels. The good angels are pure and so are allowed into the presence of God, where they praise him continually.

When were angels created? They were created at the same time as the heaven and earth, but unlike creatures of earth they have no bodies and are pure spirits.

Are there different kinds of angels? The nine ranks, or kinds, of angels are called choirs. The different choirs perform different jobs, from continually worshiping God, to carrying out his justice and performing his miracles, to being his messengers here on earth. Beginning with the highest, the ranks are seraphim, cherubim, thrones, dominions, virtues, powers, principalities, archangels, and angels.

Where did the idea of angels originate? Angelic-type spirits seem to be common to many religions around the world. But the idea of angels as we know them comes from

Mesopotamia, now called Iran. This is the land of Abraham and where the first books of the Bible were created. So angels are present in Judaism, Christianity, and Islam.

Do we worship angels? No! Angels are very popular today. Everywhere you go, you can see people with an angel pin on their shoulder or over their hearts. But we do not worship angels. They are not God; they are only servants of God. Perhaps because people saw the messenger, but not the one who sent the messenger, they became confused. This has been a problem for thousands of years. Even St. Paul in his Letter to the Colossians (chapter 2, verse 18) warned against the "worship of angels." We may pray to angels, but we pray only that they intercede for us, which means that they speak to God on our behalf. Only God alone can answer our prayers and only God alone should be worshipped.

Where do we get our information about angels? There are Jewish texts written during biblical times, like the Book of Enoch, which refers to angels. Also many saints and the early fathers of the church received revelations about the angels, which over the years have been held to be true. But some of the most important information we have about angels comes from the Bible. There are many stories about them, as well as many references to them, scattered throughout both the Old and New Testament.

Here then are the stories of angels in the Bible.

Angels in the Old Testament

1

Hagar's Hard Choice

After ten years of marriage, Sarah had not conceived a child. She suggested to her husband Abraham that he use her Egyptian handmaiden Hagar to produce the heir. Sarah would be able to call the child her own and raise it.

Hagar became pregnant and treated her mistress with scorn. Sarah complained to her husband Abraham. He responded, "But your maid is in your power. Do to her as you wish."

So Sarah whipped her maid in anger and the maid fled into the wilderness.

The angel of the Lord found Hagar by a spring of water on the way to Shur.

He said, "Hagar, maid of Sarah, where have you come from and where are you going?

She said, "I am fleeing from my mistress Sarah."

The angel of the Lord said, "Return to your mistress, and submit to her. In return I will greatly multiply your descendants so they cannot be numbered."

He continued, "Behold, you are with child, and shall bear a son; you shall call his name Ishmael, which means 'God hears,' because the Lord heard your complaints. But your son shall be like a wild ass, and he will never be at peace with his fellow men."

This was a hard choice to make, because Sarah had been so cruel to her, but Hagar returned and bore Abraham a son, and Abraham named him Ishmael.

Ten years later God was talking to Abraham and said, "As to Sarah your wife, I will bless her. She shall be a mother of nations, and kings shall come from her. She shall bear you a son, and you shall call him Isaac. I will establish my covenant with him as an everlasting covenant for his descendants after him. As for Ishmael, I will bless him too and make him fruitful. He will be the father of twelve princes, and I will make his descendants a great nation. But I will establish my covenant with Isaac, whom Sarah shall bear to you at this season next year."

Sarah overheard this conversation and ran into the tent laughing.

The Lord said to Abraham, "Why did Sarah laugh? Is anything too hard for the Lord?"

Sarah did conceive and delivered a healthy boy they named Isaac, which means "he laughs."

One day Sarah saw her son playing with Hagar's son, Ishmael, and became angry. She did not want Ishmael to get any of Isaac's inheritance. So Abraham ordered Hagar and Ishmael to leave.

Hagar and Ishmael wandered in the wilderness of Beer-sheba. Soon all their water was gone. Hagar laid her son on the ground a distance away because she did not want to see him die. Then she lay down herself, gave up hope, and began to cry. An angel of the Lord heard her.

"Don't be afraid, Hagar," he began. "The Lord has heard you. Get up, take your son's hand, and hold on tight, because he will become a great nation."

The Lord then showed Hagar where there was a well, and they survived, and Ishmael did become father to a great nation.

Genesis 16—18:15; 21

2

Sodom and Gomorrah

Abraham and God were talking one day about the problems in the neighboring cities of Sodom and Gomorrah. God was not pleased with the citizens' evil behavior.

God and Abraham argued how many innocent men it would take to make a city worthwhile.

Finally God said, "I will not destroy the city if there are ten innocent men."

But he could not find ten innocent men, only the family of Lot, Abraham's nephew.

That evening two angels showed up at the gates of Sodom where Lot was sitting. As soon as he saw the angels, he got up to meet them. Lot bowed down before them and said, "Sirs, I am here to serve you. Please come to my house. You can wash up and spend the night. In the morning you can get up early and go on your way."

The angels replied, "No, we will spend the night here in the city square."

That evening, Lot kept asking until the two angels entered his home. Soon after, there was loud banging on the door and they heard, "Where are the men who are staying with you tonight? Bring them out so we can party with them and have a good time." All the men of Sodom surrounded Lot's house.

Lot went outside to the crowd and said, "These men are guests in my home. I must protect them."

But the crowd said, "Get out of our way, you foreigner! Out of our way, or we will treat you worse than them." They wanted to break down the door. But the two angels reached out, pulled Lot back into the house, and shut the door. Then the angels struck all the men outside with blindness, so they couldn't find the door to Lot's home.

The angels said to Lot, "If you have anyone else here—son, daughter, sons-in-law, or any other relatives living in the city—get them out of town because we are going to destroy this place. The Lord has heard terrible accusations against these people and has sent us to destroy Sodom."

At dawn the angels tried to make Lot's family leave the city. They said, "Hurry up and get out of here; the Lord is going to destroy this place." Now Lot's small family didn't believe the angels and refused to leave their home.

The Lord took pity on them and told the angels to lead Lot and his family out to the city limits. One of the angels cried, "Run for your lives! Don't look back and don't stop in the valley. Run to the hills, so you won't be killed."

Suddenly the Lord rained burning sulfur on the cities of Sodom and Gomorrah, destroying them and the whole valley. All the people and everything that grew on the land died. Lot's family survived. But Lot's wife, forgetting the angel's warning, looked back at her home and was turned into a pillar of salt.

Early the next morning Abraham hurried to the place where he had stood in the presence of the Lord. He looked down at Sodom and Gomorrah and saw smoke rising from the land, like smoke from a huge furnace. But when God destroyed the cities where Lot was living, he remembered Abraham. He did not kill his nephew but allowed Lot to escape to safety with the help of his angels.

Genesis 18:16—19:29

3

Jacob's Ladder

Jacob was a great leader of the Jewish people. He lived in the land of Canaan long before Jesus was born.

When Jacob was a young man, his father, Isaac, blessed him. Then he sent Jacob away to find a wife. Isaac told Jacob, "Go, visit your Uncle Laban. He has many daughters. Maybe you can marry one of them."

The first night of his journey Jacob set up camp. He made dinner and then fell asleep resting his head on a rock. While he was sleeping, Jacob had a dream. He saw a ladder that reached from the earth to heaven. On it were many angels moving up and down the ladder. Then Jacob saw an awesome sight: God was standing at the top of the ladder looking down at him.

The Lord God spoke to Jacob. He said, "I am the God of Abraham and of your father, Isaac. The ground you are sleeping on is holy. I am giving it to you and your children and their children. I will protect you from harm and bring you here again safely."

In the morning Jacob awoke. He was filled with fear because the great God had spoken to him. "This is the House of God," he cried, "and this is the entrance to heaven!" Jacob didn't want to forget this special place. So he could find it again, he took the stone he had used for a pillow. Adding more stones, he made a tall pillar. Then he named the place "Bethel," meaning "House of God."

Before leaving, Jacob made a promise to God. "If you protect me on my journey and bring me safely back to my father's house, I will choose you as my God. I will repay you with a tenth of all I earn. And this pillar will become a place where many people will worship you." Then Jacob continued on his journey to find a wife.

Genesis 28:1–22

4

Jacob and the Angel

Jacob thought to himself, "I am so tired, I have struggled with this stranger for hours. How am I going to beat him?"

Rachel, his wife, called, "What in the world are you doing over there, Jacob? I can't see you in the dark; I just hear your panting. What is going on?"

It was many years after Jacob's dream of the ladder of angels. Jacob had found a wife and had many children. Now he was at last taking his family to meet his brother Esau who lived far away. At a river, Jacob sent his family ahead of him. They were camping on the other side of the stream and waiting for him to cross. But a man had come upon Jacob in the dark and started to wrestle with him. They wrestled all night because neither one could win.

"How am I going to beat him?" Jacob wondered.

Finally there was a glimmer of light and the other man asked Jacob, "Let me go, for the day is breaking."

Jacob replied, "Are you crazy? My children and wives and servants are on the other side of the stream. If I let you go, you may kill them."

All of a sudden, Jacob screamed. The other man had pressed the hollow of his thigh and put his hip out of joint. Jacob was sobbing when he said, "I will not let you go until you bless me."

The other man said, "What is your name?"

"Jacob."

Then the other man said, "Your name will no longer be Jacob, but Israel, for you have striven with God and with men, and have won.

Then Jacob asked, "Tell me your name."

The other man did not say his name but he finally blessed Jacob.

Jacob named the place Peniel, which means "Face of God," and told his family, "I have seen God face to face, and yet I am still alive."

The sun rose on Jacob as he limped by, passing the new river crossing called Peniel where he had struggled with an angel.

Genesis 32

5

Moses and the Towering Pillar of Cloud

The Israelites had been living in Egypt for many generations and had become slaves there. Then God raised up a leader to bring his people to freedom, up out of Egypt and back to their homeland of Israel. That leader was Moses.

Moses warned Pharaoh, the Egyptian king, to let the Israelites go. When Pharaoh refused, God sent many plagues against the Egyptians, including locusts, frogs, flies, hail, a river of blood, and finally the death of all first-born children.

Finally, Pharaoh allowed Moses to lead his people out of Egypt. But when Pharaoh realized he was losing all his servants, he soon changed his mind. He sent his army and his best chariots after the Israelites to bring them back.

The Israelites were trapped. In front of them was the Red Sea. To their right lay a vast marsh, to their left the

Mediterranean Sea, and to their back the desert—and Pharaoh's army.

Moses prayed to God and the Lord answered.

"Lift up your rod," said God, "and stretch out your hand over the Red Sea and divide it, that the people of Israel may walk on dry land between the waters."

Moses stretched out his hand; and the Lord drove the sea apart by a strong east wind.

As the Israelites walked through the sea, the angel of God appeared before them. The pillar of cloud containing the angel moved in front of them and then remained in place, eventually coming between the army of Egypt on one side and the fleeing people of Israel on the other. All night the angel in the cloud stood guard so that the Egyptian army and chariots never caught up with the fleeing Israelites.

The Israelites made it through the sea, walking on the dry path God had prepared for them, with a wall of water rising on either side. Following them, Pharaoh's army was just in the middle of the sea when Moses on the far side heard the Lord say, "Stretch out your hand over the sea, so the water can drown the Egyptians." Moses did as the Lord said and all of Pharaoh's troops were drowned.

The Israelites followed Moses into the desert where they wandered for forty years before finding the promised land of milk and honey. The cloud containing the angel moved with them until they reached Mount Sinai where Moses received the Ten Commandments. There the Lord talked with Moses and a cloud settled on the stone tablets on which the commandments were written. This time, God was in the cloud instead of the angel. God stayed with the tablets on their long journey to Jerusalem.

Moses was never to see the Promised Land in Canaan. He died as the Israelites approached the walls of Jericho, the defending city of the Canaanites.

Exodus 14:4–30

6

The Angel and the Donkey

After they escaped from Egypt, the Israelites were doing well with God's help. They had defeated their enemies and had set up camp on the plains of Moab, east of the Jordan River. Balak, the king of Moab, heard about the conquests and saw how many Israelite soldiers there were. The Moabites were worried. So Balak sent messengers and payment to a man named Balaam, who was known for being able to put curses on people. King Balak wanted Balaam to curse the Israelites.

God said to Balaam, "Do not go with these men, and do not put a curse on the people of Israel, because they have my blessing."

Three times messengers came with gold to tempt Balaam but he wouldn't go.

Finally that night God came to him and said, "If these men ask you to go with them, get ready and go, but do only what I tell you." So the next morning Balaam saddled his

donkey and went with the Moabite leaders. Perhaps Balaam was thinking about the money he would now get anyway, because God became angry that he was going.

Balaam was riding his donkey with two of his servants walking beside him, when suddenly an angel stood in their way. When the donkey saw the angel standing there holding a sword, it left the road and turned into the fields. Balaam didn't see the angel, and beat the donkey, and brought it back to the road.

Then the angel stood where the road narrowed between two vineyards with a stone wall on each side. When the donkey saw the angel, it scraped up against the wall and crushed Balaam's foot. Balaam beat him again.

Once more the angel moved ahead; he stood in a narrow place where there was no room to pass on either side. This time, when the donkey saw the angel, it lay down. Balaam lost his temper and began to beat the donkey with his stick. Then the Lord gave the donkey the power of speech. It said to Balaam, "What have I done to you? Why have you beaten me these three times?"

Balaam answered, "Because you have made a fool of me! If I had a sword, I would kill you."

The donkey replied, "Am I not the same donkey on which you have ridden all your life? Have I ever treated you like this before?"

"No," he answered.

Suddenly the Lord let Balaam see the angel standing there with his sword, and Balaam threw himself face down on the ground.

The angel demanded, "Why have you beaten your donkey three times like this? I have come to bar your way, because you should not be making this journey. But your donkey saw me and turned aside three times. If it hadn't, I would have killed you and spared the donkey."

Balaam said, "I have sinned. I will go back home."

But the angel said, "No, go. But be sure to say only what you are told to say."

And Balaam went with the men to King Balak, but instead of cursing the Israelites, Balaam blessed them, just as God told him to do.

Numbers 22

7

Elijah and the Angel of God

Elijah was a great prophet of Israel. He preached that there was only one true God. He told the people they should not worship idols made of stone or gold. But many Israelites followed the religion of Baal, a popular god of the Canaanites.

Elijah wanted to show the Jews that his God was more powerful than a man-made idol like Baal. Elijah challenged the priests of Baal to a contest. Elijah won when a bolt of lightning hit his offering and it was burnt down to the stones under the altar.

The people were amazed! They fell to their knees. They shouted, "Jehovah is God! Jehovah is God! Elijah has won over the priests of Baal. He has shown that his God is the only God. His God is the most powerful."

King Ahab of the Canaanites told Queen Jezebel what Elijah had done. The queen was a wicked woman, and she was furious to have her god defeated. She sent this

message to Elijah: "You won over my prophets. I am so mad, I am going to kill you."

Elijah ran away so as not to be murdered.

"I've had enough," he said to God. "Take away my life."

He lay down under a broom tree and fell asleep. While he was sleeping, an angel touched Elijah and told him, "Get up and eat." Elijah looked around. Bread was baking on hot stones. In a jug was water. The angel had made a meal for him. Elijah sat up and ate. Then he fell asleep again.

The angel tapped him on the shoulder again and said, "Elijah, get up and eat some more. You have a long journey ahead." The food gave Elijah the strength to walk forty days and forty nights. At last he reached Mount Horeb, the mountain of God. There Elijah found a cave to live in.

God told Elijah to come out of the cave and stand on the mountainside because he was going to pass by. First there was a mighty windstorm. All the rocks were torn loose and rolled down the sides of the mountain. But God was not in the windstorm. Then a giant earthquake shook the ground. But God was not in the earthquake. Next there was a burning fire. But God was not in the fire.

Finally Elijah heard a whisper. He went outside the entrance of his cave and wrapped his face in a cloth. Then God spoke to Elijah in a still small voice. He said, "Anoint Hazael and Jehu as kings, and anoint Elisha as your assistant." Then God left Elijah to carry out his commands.

1 Kings 19

8

The Army of Sennacherib

King Hezekiah of Judah was threatened by Sennacherib, the king of Assyria, who had defeated all the countries around them. He had already captured many of the Israelites and was coming for the rest. Sennacherib wanted the remaining Israelites to surrender without a fight. So his ambassador called out to the Judean people:

"Don't let King Hezekiah fool you. He will not be able to escape. He will tell you that his God will deliver you and that Jerusalem will not fall into our hands. Don't listen to him. Have Samaria's gods saved *them*? Why would *your* god save Jerusalem? Surrender and you won't die."

The people didn't answer the ambassador.

The leaders of the Israelites went to Jerusalem. When King Hezekiah heard what the king of Assyria had said, he tore his clothes and covered himself with sackcloth. Then he entered the temple to pray. Afterward, he sent his court officials, as well as his leading priests, all of

them also clothed in sackcloth, to Isaiah the prophet. They told Isaiah of the great insult against them, that Sennacherib had told the Israelites to turn away from the Lord God, to surrender, and to go to Assyria—or to stay and be killed.

Isaiah told them to return with this message: "The Lord God says, 'Do not be afraid. I myself will put a spirit on Sennacherib so that when he returns to Assyria, I will cause him to fall by the sword.'"

Sennacherib's ambassador returned to his king, who was busy defeating yet another country. Once he had won that battle, he sent another taunting message to King Hezekiah, saying, "You have heard what the kings of Assyria have done to *all* lands, utterly destroying them. Will *you* be saved? Where are the kings of Hamath, of Arpad, of Hena, or the king of Ivvah? They are all dead."

When King Hezekiah received this new message, he went back to the temple and prayed, "O Lord God of Israel, who are enthroned above the angels, you have made heaven and earth. Hear the words of King Sennacherib, which he has sent to mock you. Truly, the kings of Assyria *have* destroyed nations and their lands. Now, Lord, save *us,* so that all the kingdoms of the earth may know that you alone are God."

Through the prophet Isaiah, the Lord God said, yes, many cities and peoples had been destroyed by the Assyrians. But even that was part of the Lord's plan. But since Assyria had grown arrogant and because it raged in anger against God, the Lord would put a hook in Assyria's nose and a bit in its mouth, just like a farm animal, and God would turn the army back the way it came.

That very night the angel of the Lord came and struck down 185,000 men in the Assyrian camp. When morning broke, they were all dead!

King Sennacherib left at once and returned to live at Nineveh. As he was worshipping in the temple of his god Nisroch, two of his sons attacked and killed him with a sword. Then the two murderers escaped into the land of Ararat in Turkey.

But King Hezekiah lived and continued to rule the Israelites for years after this.

2 Kings 19

9

King David and the Angel of God

King David composed most of the psalms in the Bible. He also was a good king, solving problems of many men. One day King David decided he wanted to take a census to see how many Hebrews lived in Israel.

God was displeased about the census. He said to Gad, David's prophet, "Go and tell David that he may choose from among three different punishments. I will do whichever he chooses."

Gad went to the king's chambers and asked David, "Which of these will you choose to make amends with God: three years of famine, or three months of running from your enemy's army, or three days of pestilence and attack from the Lord, who will use his angel to bring death throughout Israel. Tell me which you pick so I can tell the Lord."

David replied, "I don't want to be punished by men. Let the Lord himself be the one to punish me. Because he is merciful, I take the third choice."

So the Lord sent an epidemic, and seventy thousand people in Israel died. Next he sent an angel to destroy Jerusalem, but at the last second God changed his mind and said to the angel, "Stop! That's enough!"

David saw the angel hovering in midair between heaven and earth, holding a sword in his hand, ready to destroy Jerusalem. David quickly called all of his counselors together. Wearing sackcloth, they all bowed low with their faces touching the ground. David prayed, "O God, I am the one who did wrong. I am the one who ordered the census. What have these poor people done? Lord, punish me and my family but spare your people."

The angel of the Lord told Gad, "Command David to build an altar to the Lord at this very spot, which is where Ornan and his sons are threshing wheat."

Then David announced, "This is where the temple of the Lord God will be. Here is the altar where the people of Israel are to offer burnt offerings."

David then started building the temple in Jerusalem that stood until King Nebuchadnezzar destroyed it centuries later.

1 Chronicles 21

10

Shadrach, Meshach, and Abednego

When the small Hebrew kingdom of Judah rebelled against his rule, the Chaldean King Nebuchadnezzar destroyed their temple in Jerusalem and carried several thousand Jewish captives to Babylon. His main god was Marduk.

During Nebuchadnezzar's reign he built an image of gold, sixty yards tall and six yards wide. He was very proud of his golden image and invited his governors, counselors, treasurers, justices, magistrates, and all officers of the kingdom to attend the dedication of the statue. The herald proclaimed, "You are commanded, all peoples, no matter what your nation or language, that when you hear the sound of the horn, pipe, lyre, triangle, harp, bagpipe, and choir—fall down and worship the golden image of King Nebuchadnezzar. If you do not, you will immediately be cast into a fiery furnace."

Two Chaldeans reported to their king that certain Jews working for the city of Babylon did not serve his gods or worship the golden image. Their names were Shadrach, Meshach, and Abednego. On hearing this, the king fell into a terrible rage and demanded that the three Jews be brought to him.

On their arrival Nebuchadnezzar asked them, "Is it true that you do not serve my gods or worship the golden image that I have made?" Shadrach, Meshach, and Abednego answered that they did not worship his gods, but only their one true God. Nebuchadnezzar's face turned red with anger, and he ordered the furnace heated seven times hotter than usual. Then he ordered Shadrach, Meshach, and Abednego bound and thrown into the fiery furnace. The heat pouring out of the door was so tremendous that even the soldiers standing next to the furnace were killed. As Shadrach, Meshach, and Abednego fell into the flames, they proclaimed the glory of God on High.

Looking into the furnace, King Nebuchadnezzar was astonished, and he asked his counselors, "Did we not cast three men all bound up into the fire?"

They answered, "True, O King."

He said, "But I see four men loose, walking in the middle of the fire, and they are not hurt; and the appearance of the fourth looks like a son of the gods."

Then the king came near the door of the furnace and said, "Shadrach, Meshach, and Abednego, servants of the most High God, come out of the furnace."

They emerged from the fire to stand before the king. None of them had been burned, nor their clothes, nor did they even smell of smoke.

Nebuchadnezzar said, "Blessed be the God of Shadrach, Meshach, and Abednego, who has sent his angel to deliver his servants, who trusted in him. Therefore I make a decree: Any people, no matter what their nation or language, that speaks anything against the God of Shadrach, Meshach, and Abednego shall be torn limb from limb and their houses laid waste." And he promoted Shadrach, Meshach, and Abednego into higher offices.

Daniel 3

11

Zechariah and the Red Horse

Two generations after the destruction of the temple, God came to the prophet Zechariah. He said, "I, the Lord, am very angry with your ancestors, but now I say to you, return to me, and I will return to you. Do not be like your ancestors. They would not listen to my prophets or me. Now the people have repented and acknowledged that I, the Lord Almighty, have punished them as they deserve."

Three months later, while Zechariah was asleep, the Lord gave him a message in a vision. In it, he saw an angel of the Lord riding a red horse. Behind him were other horses—red, dappled, and white. Zechariah asked him, "Sir, what do these horses mean?"

The Lord answered, "They are sent to inspect the earth. On their return they will report to the angel: 'We have been all over the world and have found it is free of war and all the lands subdued.'"

Then the angel said, "Almighty Lord, you have been angry with Jerusalem and the cities of Judah for seventy years. How much longer will it be before you show them mercy?"

The Lord answered with comforting words, "I have deep love and concern for Jerusalem, my holy city, and I am very angry with the other nations that enjoy quiet and peace. I was a little angry at my people, but those nations made their sufferings worse. Now I have come back to show mercy to Jerusalem. My temple will be restored, and the city rebuilt."

Zechariah 1

12

The Angel Raphael

Tobit was a good man, and he had a good son named Tobias.

One day Tobit remembered that many years ago he had left ten talents of silver in trust with his friend Gabael at the town of Rages in Media. As Tobit himself had become blind, he told his son to go to Rages in Media to get the silver. "Find a man to go with you," said Tobit.

Tobias found Raphael, who was an angel. Tobias did not know this and asked him, "Can you go with me to Rages in Media? Do you know that region?"

The angel replied, "I will go with you, I am familiar with the way, and I have even stayed with Gabael."

Tobias took the angel to his father, who also thought the angel was a man. Tobit asked him his tribe and family, as this stranger was to travel with his son.

Raphael said, "I am Azariah, son of the great Hananiah, one of your relatives." Tobit was pleased to hear this.

Tobias and Raphael began their journey. As they approached Ecbatana, the angel said, "Tobias, today we shall stay with Raguel. He is your relative, and he has an only daughter named Sarah. I will suggest that she be given to you in marriage."

Tobias answered, "But I've heard that Sarah has been married seven times, and at each wedding, a demon has killed her husband!"

The angel told Tobias how to frighten the demon away. "Then afterwards," said the angel, "you and Sarah should both cry out to the merciful God, and he will save you and have mercy on you. You will live and have children."

Tobias and Sarah were married, and when the demon appeared, Tobias scared it away as the angel told him to do. The demon fled to the remotest part of Egypt, but Raphael followed him there and captured him.

Tobias and Sarah then knelt down and prayed. They blessed God, prayed for safety, and asked that they be allowed to grow old together. And God heard their prayers.

After collecting the silver, Raphael led Tobias and his new wife back home to Tobit and then he healed Tobit's eyes. Tobit called to the angel and offered him half of the silver for bringing his son back safely and for restoring his sight.

The angel replied, "When you, Tobit, and your daughter-in-law prayed about your problems, I brought your prayer before the Holy One. And God sent me to heal you and Sarah. Now I can tell you: I am Raphael, one of the seven holy angels who present the prayers of the saints and enter into the presence of the glory of God."

And everyone blessed God for his marvelous deeds.

Tobit 5–12

Angels in the
New Testament

13

Mary and the Angel Gabriel

Mary was a teenager who lived in Nazareth. One day while she was praying, the angel Gabriel appeared to her. The angel was very tall and light shone all around him. Gabriel said to her, "Hail, Mary! Full of grace! The Lord is with you!"

Mary was shocked at the sight. "What have I done that you have come to visit me?" she asked quietly.

Gabriel answered, "God has chosen you to be the mother of his son."

"Me?" replied Mary. "But how can that be? I am not even married."

"The Holy Spirit will come upon you," replied the angel, "and you will be known as special among all women. Your baby will be the Messiah who shall save the world."

Then Mary said, "Yes, I will do as God asks. I am the servant of the Lord."

And the
angel Gabriel
disappeared.

Mary was
puzzled about what
the angel had told her.
She kept the visit a secret.

One day Mary went to visit her
cousin Elizabeth, who was much
older than Mary. After forty years of
marriage, Elizabeth had no children.
But an angel had visited her husband
Zechariah and told him they were going to have a son. The
cousins Mary and Elizabeth were astonished that both of
them had been visited by the angel Gabriel!

Elizabeth's son was born. She and her husband
Zechariah named him John, just as the angel told them to,
and the baby grew up to be John the Baptist.

Mary's son was born in a stable, and she named him
Jesus.

Luke 1

14

Joseph's Dilemma

Joseph was engaged to Mary. One day she asked Joseph to sit down and she told him what had happened. Mary said, "An angel came to me. He said that I was going to have a baby and that the baby was the Son of God."

Joseph was shocked and did not believe the story. He loved Mary and decided a quiet divorce would be best. They would break the engagement and tell only their families.

That same night an angel visited Joseph. The angel said, "Joseph, son of David, do not fear to take Mary as your wife, for what is conceived in her is of the Holy Spirit. She will bear a son, and shall call him Jesus, for he will save his people from their sins." Then the angel disappeared. Joseph was happy to raise such a special son.

Nine months later Mary delivered her son. She and Joseph named him Jesus. He was born far from home in Bethlehem, where there was no place to lay the child except a manger.

A short time later, an angel again appeared to Joseph and warned him that his family was in danger. Soldiers were coming from King Herod to kill the baby! Joseph got up in the middle of the night and took Mary and Jesus, and they fled to Egypt. They stayed there until the angel appeared one more time. This time the angel told Joseph that it was safe to return. The wicked king who had wanted to kill Jesus was now dead.

So Joseph took Jesus and Mary and returned home to Israel, and they settled in Mary's hometown of Nazareth.

Matthew 1:18—2

15

Angels of Bethlehem

The night that Jesus was born, shepherds were in the field watching their flocks to ensure the safe birth of their lambs. It was a beautiful, clear night and the sky was bright with stars. Suddenly angels fluttered above them, singing "Alleluia!" An angel of the Lord appeared to them, and the glory of the Lord shone around them with a great light. The shepherds were terrified and fell down.

The angel of the Lord said to them in a sweet tinkling voice, "Do not be afraid. I bring you good news of great joy that will be for all the people. Today in the town of Bethlehem, a Savior has been born to you; he is Christ the Lord. This will be a sign to you: you will find the baby wrapped in swaddling cloths and lying in a manger."

Suddenly a great company of the heavenly host appeared with the angel, praising God and saying,

"Glory to God in the highest,
And on earth peace to men of good will."

When the angels had disappeared, the shepherds said to one another, "Let's go to Bethlehem and see what the Lord has done."

In the distance the shepherds saw a huge gleaming star, which led them to the stable. There they discovered the baby Jesus lying in the manger wrapped in swaddling clothes.

The shepherds fell to their knees and worshipped the newborn Son of God.

Luke 2:8–15

16

The Temptation of Jesus

Jesus was baptized by his cousin John in the Jordan River. Afterwards the heavens opened, and the Spirit of God descended in the shape of a dove. And God said, "This is my Son, whom I love. With him I am well pleased."

Right after the baptism, the Spirit led Jesus into the desert to be tempted by the devil. Jesus did not eat for forty days and forty nights, and he was hungry.

Then the devil appeared and said, "If you are the Son of God, tell these stones to become bread."

Jesus answered, "It is written: One does not live on bread alone, but on every word that comes from the mouth of God."

Next the devil took him to the holy city of Jerusalem and had him stand on the highest point of the temple and said, "If you are the Son of God, throw yourself down. For it is written that God will command his angels to protect you and you won't even strike your foot against a stone."

Jesus answered, "It is also written: Do not put the Lord your God to the test."

Finally the devil took him to a very high mountain and showed him all the kingdoms of the world and their splendor. "All this I will give you," the devil said, "if you will bow down and worship me."

Jesus said to him, "Away from me, Satan! For it is written: Worship the Lord your God, and serve him only"

Then the devil left, and angels came and waited on Jesus.

Matthew 4

17

Angels of the Resurrection

Three days after Jesus was crucified, Mary Magdalene and Mary the mother of James went to the tomb where the Lord had been laid. As the women approached the tomb, there was a sudden earthquake. An angel from heaven rolled away the heavy stone at the entrance to the tomb. Then the angel sat down on the stone. His face was like lightning and his clothes looked white as snow. The soldiers guarding the tomb were terrified. They fell on their faces to the ground. Then they ran away.

When the women saw the angel, they were frightened too. But the angel said, "Don't be afraid. I know you are looking for the body of Jesus who was crucified." Then the angel told them, "Jesus is not here. He has risen from the dead. Come inside the tomb and see where he was laid." The two Marys entered the tomb and saw that it was empty.

The angel then told them, "Go quickly, and tell the disciples that the Lord has risen from the dead. He has gone to Galilee. You will see Jesus there."

The women were happy and excited, but they were also confused. They found Peter and John, and cried out, "Someone has taken Jesus' body. We don't know where they have put him."

The disciples ran toward the tomb. John arrived first and stooped down to look inside. All he saw were burial clothes lying on the ground. Peter arrived panting. Both men were as confused as the women. They remembered that Jesus told them he would be killed and on the third day rise from the dead. But they hadn't really believed that was possible. Now they did.

The disciples named that wonderful day *Easter*. It became the greatest feast day of the Church. Now all Christians celebrate that amazing event, the day our Lord rose from the dead.

Matthew 28, John 20

18

Philip and the Ethiopian Official

Philip, one of the twelve apostles, saw an angel of the Lord, who said, "Get ready and go south to the road that leads from Jerusalem to Gaza." So Philip got ready and left.

On that same day, an Ethiopian official in charge of the treasury of the Queen of Ethiopia was on his way home. He had been to Jerusalem to worship God and was going back to his mountain home in his carriage. As he rode along, he read from the book of the prophet Isaiah.

The angel of the Lord said to Philip, "Go over to that carriage and stay close to it."

Philip ran over and heard the official reading from the book of Isaiah. Philip asked him, "Do you understand what you are reading?"

The Ethiopian replied, "How can I understand unless someone explains it to me?" And he invited Philip to climb up and sit in the carriage with him. The passage of scripture that he was reading was this:

"He was like a sheep that is taken to be slaughtered.
 And like a lamb that makes no sound when its wool is cut off,
  he didn't say a word.
He was humiliated, and justice was denied him.
 No one will be able to tell about his descendants,
  because his life on earth has come to an end."

The official asked Philip, "Tell me, who is the prophet talking about? About himself or about someone else?"

Then Philip began to speak. Beginning with this passage of scripture, he told him the good news about Jesus.

As they traveled down the road, they came to a river. The Ethiopian said, "Here is some water. What is to keep me from being baptized?"

The official ordered the carriage to stop, and both Philip and the Ethiopian went down into the water, where Philip baptized him. When they came up out of the water, the angel of the Lord carried Philip away, so that he disappeared from sight. The official did not see him again, but continued on his way, full of joy. Philip found himself in Azotus; he went on to Caesarea, and on the way he preached the good news in every town.

Acts 8:26–40

19

Cornelius and the Angel

Cornelius was a Roman centurion stationed in Caesarea. He was a very good man, kind to his soldiers and generous to the poor. He was a Gentile, meaning he was not a Jew, but he believed in God and prayed to him every day.

One afternoon Cornelius had a vision of an angel. The angel came toward him, saying, "Cornelius! God has seen your charity and heard your prayers. He wants you to send some of your soldiers to find a man named Simon Peter. He is staying in Joppa with Simon the tanner. Have the soldiers ask Peter to come here and talk to you."

Then the angel disappeared as mysteriously as he had come. Cornelius called two of his servants and one of his soldiers and sent them off to Joppa.

When the men sent by Cornelius arrived at Joppa, they knocked on Peter's gate. Peter went downstairs, opened the gate, and said, "I'm the man you are looking for. What do you want?" The visitors told Peter about Cornelius and the angel.

Simon Peter and the visitors arrived the next day in Caesarea. Cornelius invited all his friends and relatives to come over and meet Peter, the famous Christian speaker. When Simon Peter entered the house, Cornelius dropped to his knees before the apostle, who had spent three years with Jesus. But Peter made him stand up, saying, "Get up. I'm only a man."

Peter said, "All of you know that it is against Jewish law for me to enter the house of a Gentile. But God has shown me in a vision that I should never consider anyone inferior. That's why I came when you sent for me. Now tell me what you want from me."

Cornelius asked, "Can Gentiles become Christians?" He asked this question because in the beginning only Jews were the first Christians.

Peter answered him, "God does not have favorites. He loves all people the same, no matter what their race or color or religion. He sent Jesus to be Lord of all and to save all people, and he sent me to preach the Gospel to all persons, not just the Jews."

While Peter was telling the group about Jesus and the good news of his resurrection, the Holy Spirit fell on everyone in the house. The Jews who had come with Peter were amazed. They didn't know that the Holy Spirit would fall on Gentiles, too! But the Gentiles were also speaking in tongues, prophesying, and praising God.

Then Peter baptized Cornelius and everyone in his household. Peter realized that the sacrifice of Jesus on the cross was for everyone, both Jews and non-Jews. After that the apostles started to carry the Gospel to all people throughout the vast Roman Empire.

Acts 10

20

Peter in Prison

Forty days after Jesus rose from the dead, he ascended into heaven. His disciples continued preaching and teaching in Jerusalem. Peter, who was one of the first disciples, stayed in Jerusalem even when some of the disciples went to other cities.

King Herod did not like these new Christians. First he executed James, the brother of John. Next he planned to kill Peter and so ordered him arrested.

Peter was found and placed in prison where he was chained between two guards. Two more guards were posted outside his cell to make sure he could not escape. Herod planned to execute him the next morning.

That night Peter lay asleep on the floor of the cold, dark cell. Suddenly a bright light filled the room. A tall angel appeared beside Peter. The angel put the guards to sleep. Then he struck Peter on the shoulder and said, "Peter, wake up!"

Peter rubbed his eyes, not sure of what he was seeing. "Who is that?"

"I am a messenger of God sent to help you," replied the angel.

Peter could hardly believe his ears. His eyes were dazzled by the angel's brightness.

The angel said, "Put on your cloak and shoes and follow me."

"How can I?" asked Peter. "My hands are bound with chains."

Suddenly the chains fell off his wrists and clattered to the floor. Then Peter did as the angel commanded and put on his cloak and shoes.

The angel added, "Follow me."

Peter and the angel slipped quietly past the guards and other cells. When they came to the iron gate of the prison, it suddenly swung open. They were free! After accompanying Peter a few blocks, the angel disappeared. Peter hurried to the other disciples and told them what the Lord had done for him.

Peter was the head of the brand new Christian church and is considered to be its first pope. His remains are buried under the high altar of St. Peter's Basilica in Rome.

Acts 12

21

Herod and the Angel of Death

Judea at the time of Christ was under the rule of Rome, and King Herod was its political puppet. The king was a wicked man, and his son and his grandson—also called Herod in the Bible—were just as wicked. Together they made many problems for Jesus and his followers.

When Jesus was born, three wise men stopped in Jerusalem on their way to Bethlehem and told Herod that a new king had been born. Herod wanted to be king himself. So he ordered that all boys under the age of two be killed. But Jesus escaped. An angel told Joseph to take his family and flee to Egypt till it was safe.

When Jesus grew older, his cousin John the Baptist began to tell people to repent because the Kingdom of God was coming. Herod's son did not like the things John was saying and had him beheaded.

After Jesus died and rose from the dead, the grandson was now king. This Herod put James, the brother of

John, to death. This Herod also had Peter arrested, but Peter was set free by an angel of the Lord. Herod was so angry when Peter escaped that he had the prison guards put to death.

Afterward, Herod left Jerusalem to spend some time in Caesarea. At the time he was angry with the cities of Tyre and Sidon, which were both situated on the Mediterranean Sea. A group of citizens from those cities came to see Herod. They asked him for peace, because they depended on Judea, Herod's country, for their food.

On the day of the audience, Herod put on his royal robes, sat on his throne, and made a speech to the people.

"It isn't a man speaking, but a god!" they shouted, trying to please the king.

Herod should have said, "No, I am just a man," but instead he kept the honor that was due God.

At once an angel of the Lord struck Herod down, and he was eaten by worms and died.

Acts 12:20–23

22

Paul on a Sinking Ship

St. Paul once hated Christians and spent his time arresting and killing them. But after Jesus appeared to him on the road to Damascus, Paul had a sudden conversion. Now a Christian himself, he traveled everywhere, preaching about Jesus and converting Jews and non-Jews. This made the Jewish leaders angry, and they asked the Roman governor to arrest Paul. But Paul was a Roman citizen. He could be condemned to death only by a Roman court. So he was put in chains to be sent to Rome for trial.

It was a long voyage from Israel to Italy. There were almost three hundred people on board altogether—sailors, Roman soldiers, passengers, and prisoners, including Paul. The ship sailed for several months until it reached the port of Fair Haven. By then it was winter. Most ships didn't sail during the winter because of rough, dangerous seas. But despite this and despite St. Paul's warning, the captain decided to keep sailing anyway.

During the night a howling wind arose and blew the helpless ship before it. Hoping to lighten the ship, the

sailors threw the cargo overboard, then the spare tackle and spars. But it didn't help. The sky stayed pitch black for days, and the captain couldn't see the sun or stars to steer by. Everyone gave up hope of surviving.

Over the howling wind and pounding seas, Paul shouted, "You should have listened to me and not set sail from Crete. Then you would not be in this deadly storm. But don't give up hope—not one life will be lost. Only the ship will go down."

He explained: "Last night an angel of God came to me and told me that I had to be taken before Caesar for my trial. God would save me, and everyone on the ship with me. So cheer up, because I believe what the angel said will happen. However, our ship will wash up on an island and be wrecked."

The ship continued to be tossed wildly for fourteen more days. At midnight on the fourteenth day, the sailors threw out the sounding stone and discovered the water was only 120 feet deep. This meant they were close to shore. They threw out the anchor to keep the ship from crashing onto the rocks. Then the sailors let down the lifeboat to escape.

But Paul shouted over the wind, "If you don't stay with the ship, no one will be saved. If you follow my advice, not one of you will die or even be injured!" The men stayed with the ship. The captain saw a bay ahead and tried to steer toward it and toward safe anchorage. But the ocean currents tossed the ship, and it began to break apart in the waves.

The soldiers said, "Let's kill all the prisoners so they don't swim away and escape."

But the centurion in charge wouldn't allow it. He had been told to bring Paul safely to Rome. He ordered everyone to jump overboard, whether he could swim or not. Some swam, others held onto boards from the wrecked ship. Eventually all three hundred men made it to shore.

The angel had told Paul the truth. Everyone on board that ship was saved. Later Paul continued his trip to Rome, where he was martyred for his faith.

Acts 27

23

Angels from the Revelation of John

While John was in a cave on the island of Patmos, he had a vision. He heard a loud voice that sounded like a trumpet, speaking behind him. It said, "Write down what you see, and send the book to the churches in these seven cities: Ephesus, Smyrna, Pergamum, Thyatira, Sardis, Philadelphia, and Laodicea."

John turned around and saw seven gold lamp stands. Among them there was one like the Son of Man, wearing a robe down to his feet. A gold band was around his chest. His hair was white as wool, and his eyes blazed like fire. His feet shone like polished brass, and his voice sounded like a roaring waterfall. He held seven stars in his right hand, and a sharp two-edged sword came out of his mouth. His face was bright as the midday sun.

He placed his right hand on John, who had fallen at his feet, and said, "Don't be afraid! I am the first and the last. I am the living one! I was dead, but now I am alive forever and ever. I have authority over death and the world of the dead. Write, then, the things you see, both things that are now and the things to come. The seven stars in my hand are the angels of the seven churches and the seven lamp stands are the seven churches."

It was Jesus, and he told John to write down messages for each of the angels of the seven cities.

Then the seven angels blew their horns and seven different catastrophes occurred in the world. John saw another mighty angel coming down out of heaven. This angel was wrapped in a cloud and had a rainbow around his head; his face was like the sun, and his legs like columns of fire. A small scroll was open in his hand. He put his right foot on the sea and his left foot on the land of the island and called out in a loud voice that sounded like the roar of lions. Seven thunders answered with a roar. The angel said to keep the thunders secret and not to write them down.

The angel told John to eat the scroll and then to proclaim God's message to many nations, races, languages, and kings.

John's vision continued, revealing more angels, beasts, a woman clothed with the sun, a great battle in heaven, the defeat of the devil, the resurrection of the dead, the new Jerusalem, and the end of time when Jesus returns.

At the end of the vision, John fell down at the feet of the angel. But the angel said, "Don't do that! I am only a fellow servant like you. Don't worship me. Worship God."

Revelation 1–22